God's Promises for Doubt-Filled Days

GRAHAM

P.O. Box 799070
Dallas, TX 75379
1-800-414-7693 (1-800-414-POWER)
jgraham@powerpoint.org
jackgraham.org

Unless otherwise indicated, Scripture verses quoted are
taken with permission from the English Standard Version.

IT WAS SUMMERTIME in 1970, and I was visiting the tiny town of Crowell, Texas, which seemed like the backside of nowhere to a young man from the thriving metroplex known as Dallas-Fort Worth. I was a new pastor then, and I was in the middle of preaching a youth revival when I received a call from my brother with the type of news nobody ever wants to hear. "Jack," he said, "you need to come to Fort Worth. Our dad has been hurt. He has been hit with a hammer."

My mind reeled. *A hammer?* Dad had a hardware store, but I couldn't imagine what had gone wrong.

As I made arrangements to travel back home, my heart felt deflated and weak. I'd always thought my dad would be around forever, that he was indestructible and powerful and incapable of being harmed. Maybe every son feels like that about his dad. I surely did about mine.

When I was a kid growing up in small-town Arkansas, my dad had a drive-in called the Dan-Dee-Dog. I spent countless hours chasing him around that establishment, doing my level best as a toddler to "help" him whenever possible. My efforts didn't frustrate him; instead, they elicited a smile.

All through the week, Dad tended to the innumerable responsibilities involved in running a restaurant, but come Sunday, he shut things down and took our family to church. Profits could wait; Sunday was for honoring the Sabbath. It was important to him. God mattered to him. As did his kids: my dad never missed one of my ballgames, he was never too tired to play catch and he always boasted about how proud he was of me.

...moments later, my life—life for *everyone* in my family—was about to dramatically change.

When I was 10, my father moved our family to Fort Worth, where he began working in the hardware business. And then, years later, that fateful afternoon in the summer of 1970 arrived, when I found myself standing in a pulpit, preaching the Word of God, having no idea that moments later, my life—life for *everyone* in my family—was about to dramatically change.

When the whole story finally came out, I learned that a shoplifter who had stolen from my father's store and then was caught red-handed chose to bludgeon my dad to death with a hammer. Right there in the parking lot of Buddy's Hardware.

My father lived for ten days following that horrific incident. And then my hero died.

The night that Dad passed from this reality into the reality of heaven, I walked into his room at Harris Methodist Hospital, I gripped his hand, and I asked him to please squeeze back. Ever so faintly, I felt his hand slowly tighten around mine. When I walked out that night, I thought, "That is the last time I will ever see my dad alive."

Later that evening, I made my way downstairs to the hospital's small chapel. In the darkness of that space, and weighed down by the unbelievable loss I'd soon have to bear, I sat down and buried my head in my hands. My *Leave It to Beaver* family—characterized by simple happiness, innocence, and love—was now the victim of violent crime. Of *murder*. The blissfulness of my upbringing seemed shrouded in ugliness and sin.

It was the most devastating moment of my life, and yet I knew I wasn't facing the darkness alone. God was with me. In that chapel, He was with me. And in the broader context of my life, He was near. God was an important part of my life prior to that night in the chapel of Harris Methodist Hospital, but it was in the stillness of that small room that I surrendered to Him the *entirety* of who I was. On the heels of that time of prayer, I knew He'd be my sure and steady Comforter as the storm clouds gathered in my life. Despite the seemingly unbearable pain of losing my dad far too early, God would reveal a rainbow in the midst of the rain.

⋘

Recently, I was at Rangers Ballpark in Arlington for a Texas Rangers baseball game, and as is common in this part of the country, midway through the afternoon, a hefty storm rolled in. Lightning sprinted across the sky, thunder rocked the airwaves, and rain pelted everything in sight. But then, just as the fat drops began to thin, both ends of a vibrant rainbow came into view, a divine photograph developing right before my eyes. I sat there for several minutes to take in the splendor of that rainbow and consider with fresh appreciation God's covenant promise with His people, that He would be faithful to them all of their days.

It's a promise you and I both need still, given the challenges "these days" tend to present.

I'm sure you've noticed that ours is a wounded world. Planet Earth is in pain—*real* pain, given that the Scriptures liken it to a mother enduring the rigors of labor. Granted, I haven't experienced childbirth firsthand, but from what I hear, it's no walk in the park.

Terrorism threatens every major city on the planet, natural disasters all too frequently make headlines, and from the look of things, wars will be with us for as long as humans are alive. Add to that reality the fact that experts believe our world's non-renewable resources will be exhausted within a century if we don't take dramatic action, and you've got a clear picture of a planet that is not evolving, but devolving. No wonder God's Word likens the situation to urgent and intense groans of pain.

Like mine, your life has probably proven what Scripture says, that in this world we will face trouble...

I've read that some ten thousand people in our world die each week of starvation. That's almost fifteen hundred a day—almost sixty every single hour—from lack of food alone. Others suffer from diseases spread by dirty drinking water, and still others wrestle with physical disabilities or with economic downturns or with the pain of marital strife.

Indeed, pain is global. But it's terribly local too. Like mine, your life has probably proven what Scripture says, that in this world we will face trouble—trials and difficulties and death, of a dream, of a relationship, of a loved one, of hope itself. It is in those moments when the bottom falls out that you and I both wonder how we'll survive. We doubt God's presence and His care. We doubt our ability to overcome the trial. We doubt that we'll ever move on. But a person cannot doubt what he doesn't first believe. And it is our fundamental belief in God—in His power, His presence, and His desire for good to prevail—that eventually paves the path to better days.

John 11 tells of a first-century family that Jesus loved very much. Mary, Martha, and Lazarus—two sisters and a brother—were intimate with Jesus, often spending time in His presence to learn from Him, love Him, and share life as good friends do.

It is our fundamental belief in God—in His power, His presence, and His desire for good to prevail—that eventually paves the path to better days.

The text says that one day Lazarus fell ill, and Jesus—the obvious One who could heal him—was nowhere to be found. Word was sent to Jesus that the man he loved like a brother was dying, but surprisingly, He went on about His day ministering in Jerusalem. Even though Lazarus clearly needed Him. Even though the situation was dire.

The rest of the story involves Jesus making His way to Bethany—where Lazarus's body had lain lifeless for four days straight—in His own time and on His own terms, and then miraculously raising His friend from the dead. But the point I want to make is that having a close, personal relationship with Jesus Christ did not exempt this beloved family from walking through deep pain and loss. Mary and Martha must have had their fair share of "Why, God? Why?" moments between when their brother died and when his life was amazingly restored. Didn't their Savior know their hearts were breaking? Didn't He care that their loved one was gone? Maybe God wasn't as good or as great as they'd once believed Him to be.

X

In a recent poll, people were surveyed to find out what they would ask God, if they could get just one question answered. The most common response—by a landslide—was, "Why do bad things happen to good people?" The argument behind the question goes something like this: "If there really is a God, and He really is all-knowing, all-powerful, loving and caring and kind, then how could He possibly allow pain and suffering to occur? Could it be that He isn't *actually* powerful enough to do anything about the challenges we face in this life? Or maybe He isn't as kind as everyone makes Him out to be. Either God is good, but powerless to overcome evil, or else He is powerful and mighty but just refuses to cause things to change. Either way, it's bad news regarding this allegedly 'good' God."

Even the most devoted Christ-followers come up against the raw edge of life from time to time and find themselves flirting with logic like that. "Why, God? *Why?*" they plead, wondering whether God sees them, whether He hears them, whether He cares. And no pat answer, Christian cliché, contrived solution, or seemingly air-tight formula suffices when what is craved most is the unmistakable presence of God. It was true for Mary and Martha more than two thousand years ago, and it remains true for us today.

It took a while for me to see the rainbow in the rainstorm of my dad's death, but eventually it showed up in the form of reassurance I desperately needed, reassurance I found in the book of James. Chapter one says this: "If any of you lacks wisdom, let him ask God, who gives generously to all without reproach, and it will be given him. But let him ask in faith, with no doubting, for the one who doubts is like a wave of the sea that is driven and tossed by the wind. For that person must not suppose that he will receive anything from the Lord; he is a double-minded man, unstable in all his ways."[1]

Interestingly, those verses come immediately after the well-known explanation of the good that is birthed from pain: "Count it all joy, my brothers, when you meet trials of various kinds, for you know that the testing of your faith produces steadfastness. And let steadfastness have its full effect, that you may be perfect and complete, lacking in nothing" (v. 2-4).

> **If you are alive, you *will face adversity*. As much as we would like to, Christians don't get a pass on pain.**

Note that James says, "when" you meet trials of various kinds, not "if." In other words, if you are alive, you *will face adversity*. As much as we would like to, Christians don't get a pass on pain. And while we may never discover the *whys* behind tough stuff we face in this life, based on that instructive passage, God confirms that we can *fully* know the "how." We can rest in the knowledge of how we will respond to pain and deal with our doubts. We can actually "count it all joy."

---

[1] All Scriptures ESV.

Promise #1: "I will increase your wisdom."

So, back to the "rainbow" God revealed to me long after my dad had died. It came in three parts, based on that first passage in James we looked at—three promises I could cling to on life's most difficult and doubt-filled days. The first divine promise that came into view was, "I will increase your wisdom."

Years ago I wrote these words in the margin of my Bible: "Unless there is within us that which is above us, we will soon yield to that which is around us." God's wisdom resides "above," but it can also reside *within*. We don't have to settle for a horizontal vantage point that only takes in what our eyes can see. We can instead insist on living with a *vertical* perspective, which considers God's perfect point of view. I was talking to my son Josh about wisdom recently, and he said that wisdom is like a football player who not only possesses the necessary know-how regarding the plays he is supposed to run, but who also *executes* those plays on the field in such a way that he helps to win the game. It's a fitting analogy. You and I can do much more than rack up a bunch of head-knowledge about the Christian faith; we can actually *apply* that knowledge in our daily lives. When the battering waves of difficult days cause us to tremble, to fear, and to doubt, wisdom says, "You can prevail here. You can *win* at the game called life."

So, how do we obtain this marvelous gift of wisdom? According to James 1, we simply ask. Remember verse 5, which says, "If any of you lacks wisdom, *let him ask God*, who gives generously to all without reproach, and it will be given him."[2] When the questions of life outnumber the answers, we can come to God and say, "I can't see my way through here. The waves are crashing in on me, and I'm afraid they'll pull me under!" God promises to answer a prayer like that—re-read the second part of verse 5 for proof. When we ask God for His wisdom and His perspective on life, He promises to give it to us—and to do so generously. Without reproach. Without shame or blame or even an ounce of condemnation.

When I was a young boy in school, I was often too intimidated to raise my hand and ask the teacher a question. I figured I was the only student who didn't know the answer, and I was afraid that I'd look foolish and the other kids would laugh at me. Worse yet, I didn't want the teacher to look at me with disapproving eyes and say, "Where have you *been* the last two weeks?" Thankfully, God never responds that way. When you and I come to our heavenly Father, admit our need, and request His intervention, we do well to remember that we are talking to a good God, a gracious God, a loving God who is not put off by our doubts. Faithfulness

---

[2] Emphasis added.

is synonymous with His character; He cannot not be faithful to us. It is for this reason that when we ask God for increased wisdom, we can be sure that He will meet our need. When we say honestly, "God, I don't understand. I don't have the answers, and I don't know where to turn," He embraces us instead of rejecting us. He welcomes us instead of casting us aside.

> **Overflowing, spilling out in abundance—*this* is how God wants His wisdom to characterize our lives.**

God has always been kind and always *will be* kind in future days. He is the God in whom there is no variation, no shadow due to change, as James 1:17 says. And He is always *gentle* in His response. In fact, the meaning behind James's description of God providing wisdom to us "liberally" refers to a stretching-out or a spreading-out. It's the image of a lavish banquet table, complete with every imaginable delicacy. Overflowing, spilling out in abundance—*this* is how God wants His wisdom to characterize our lives.

ᛉ

The story is told in the book of 1 Kings of a young boy named Solomon inheriting the throne of his father, David. Solomon loved God and did his best to walk in godliness, but when he was given the weight of reigning over an entire kingdom, he knew he was in over his head. During a dream one night, God appeared to Solomon and said, "Ask what I shall give you." Can you imagine God giving you a free pass like that? "Ask *anything* of me, and I'll give it to you immediately." It must have felt like a gift straight from heaven.

Solomon could have requested great riches, great power, success as king and more. But the one thing he asked of the Lord was *wisdom*. He said, "Give your servant therefore an understanding mind to govern your people, that I may discern between good and evil, for who is able to govern this your great people?"[3]

The young king knew that in order to live his life effectively, he would need a healthy dose of God's wisdom, His will, His ways. I can certainly relate. On more occasions than I can count as a pastor, I've pleaded with God for wisdom. I have come up against more than my share of leadership conundrums, and each time, my prayer is the same: "God, I can't figure this out on my own. I need Your wisdom here..."

Time and again, when it seems there is no way out of the

---

[3] 1 Kings 3:9

situation I find myself in, God finds a way. His perfect peace shows up, and His wisdom prevails. Isaiah 50:10 says, "Let him who walks in darkness and has no light trust in the name of the Lord and rely on his God." When you and I face our most challenging crossroads, may we be as candid and courageous as Solomon, who was wise enough to look heavenward for help. There is nothing more pleasing to the ears of a dad than to hear his child say, "Daddy, could you please come here? I need you." Your heavenly Father loves and longs to hear those words too.

Promise #2: "I'll replace your doubt with faith."

Years ago, when my wife, Deb, and I lived in West Palm Beach, Florida, she was asked by friends of ours to sing at their wedding. The couple had dreamed of having a sunrise ceremony near the Atlantic Ocean, so at four o'clock one Saturday morning, Deb and I dragged our weary bodies out of bed, grudgingly tugged on itchy attire, and made our way down to the beach.

When we arrived, Deb was escorted to a long jetty where she would stand for her solo. At least she was allowed to stand on a dry surface; the couple had chosen to take their vows while barefoot in the shallow surf! Even so, the constant lapping of the ocean against the shore, mixed with Deb's proneness toward motion sickness, made for one queasy vocalist. But my wife was a trouper. She pulled it together, and by the time she was due to sing, her stomach had settled, her shoulders were back, and her chin was held high.

Everything was going just as planned: The bride looked stunning in her white linen dress, the groom was beaming as he eyed the woman by his side, and my wife was hitting every note. But then, just as Deb began her final verse, the picturesque wedding scene lost a little of its charm. An uncharacteristically large wave crashed against the jetty and doused her from her perfectly styled hair to her precariously high heels. My soggy wife finished her song, but not before being reminded of just how unpredictable waves can be.

James 1 not only tells us that we can ask for wisdom when we're facing struggles in life, but also how to make "the ask." Verse six says that we are to ask *in faith*—with no doubting, because "he who doubts is like a wave in the sea, driven and tossed by the wind." In other words, when we request wisdom from God, we must stand firm in anticipation of a positive response. We must ask with predictable confidence instead of wavering like the wind-whipped sea.

The apostle Simon Peter learned this lesson firsthand. Late one night, while Peter and the other disciples were at sea, Jesus appeared to them walking on the water. The disciples were terrified because they thought they were seeing a ghost, but Jesus quickly allayed their fears. Still, to test whether it really was Jesus standing there on the sea, Peter said, "Lord, if it's you, tell me to come to you on the water."[4]

Jesus in essence said, "Well, step on out!"

So, Simon stood up in the boat, placed his feet overboard, and began to walk toward Jesus. He did fine as long as he fixed his gaze on Christ. But as soon as he turned his attention to the wind, the waves, the water surrounding him, he began to sink. "What am I doing here?" he probably thought. "I can't *walk on water!* But I believe I'm doing it now! No, wait: I *don't* believe. Well, do I believe I can do this, or not?"

Peter was in the presence of the omnipotent Christ, and yet he focused on his troubling circumstances instead. But before you judge him to be a faithless fisherman, keep in mind that he walked further on water than you or I ever will. What's more, I bet you can relate as well as I can to his predicament. We don't want to doubt God's ability to help us in our time of need, but sometimes it's hard to keep from turning our challenges over and over in our minds like a broken record that spins around and yet never gets anywhere in the end. We take our eyes off of Jesus, the Source of our faith. And just like Simon Peter, we start to go down.

---

[4] Matthew 14:27

Thankfully, we can choose another way. We can lean into the flawless, unfailing wisdom of God that promises buoyancy for even our most turbulent days.

After my dad died, I desperately needed that type of steadiness in my storm. The natural reaction to losing a family member to violent crime is rage and a boatload of blame—toward the murderer, toward the criminal-justice system, sometimes even toward God. But very quickly I realized if I let hatred and bitterness take root in my soul, I would be the one suffering for years to come. Romans 8 says "those who are led by the Spirit of God are the sons of God" and that "the Spirit helps us in our weakness" (vv. 14, 26). I knew the Spirit of God was asking me to forgive, and while I didn't *feel* like forgiving the man who cut my dad's life short, I acted on the belief that God was and is the ultimate judge, and that my job was to forgive. That willful act of simple surrender, fueled by wisdom from above, freed me from further anger and invited healing to run its course in my life.

Your situation may not involve the tragic loss of a loved one but instead financial pain, marital pain, occupational pain, or some other struggle entirely. Regardless of your circumstances, you face the same choice that I did: Will you take your eyes off of Jesus and sink, or will you allow God's presence and power to steady you for the storm?

We need to learn how to doubt our doubts and believe our beliefs. But granted, it's easier said than done.

More than a year ago, I stood in my living room with a phone in my hand and heard these words from the doctor on the other end: "You have prostate cancer." Admittedly, I was shocked. Cancer is something I thought happened to other people but would never happen to me. And yet there it was, in four simple words, the diagnosis I couldn't deny.

> **I had preached God's promises for three decades' time, and now I faced a magnificent opportunity to prove whether I believed them or not.**

The months that followed were stuffed full with every conceivable emotion, but through it all, Deb and I determined that we would trust God. We would not doubt His care for me or His promise of provision in future days. Instead of asking *Why me?* I asked *Why* not *me?* All I could think about was how I had preached God's promises for three decades' time, and now I faced a magnificent opportunity to prove whether I believed them or not.

Not surprisingly, God has been faithful to walk by my side each step of the way. The cancer, thankfully, is now gone, but even if that physical battle still raged, I would testify to the faithfulness of God. He doesn't always deliver rosy outcomes when we face challenges in this life. But He *does* always stay present, exchanging each ounce of doubt with faith.

I often tell the congregation at Prestonwood that I think aside from the name of Jesus, the most oft-repeated word uttered in heaven will be "Aha!" I envision us walking around those streets of gold saying, "Aha! So, *that's* what that was all about. *That's* why I went through those dark days. *That's* why my life took the turn that it did...." If you frequently catch yourself eyeing the sky and asking God why, then take a closer look at your posture in prayer. Are you hunched over in defeat, praying from a place of doubt? Or are you boldly coming before God's throne, claiming His great promises by sure and steady faith? I hope you don't settle for a wind-whipped life, a life characterized primarily by doubt. In *Pilgrim's Progress,* author John Bunyan called this type of individual Mr. Facing-Both-Ways, but double-mindedness doesn't need to mark you. Instead, you can live with the singular focus that God sees, He knows, and He cares.

X

When I was a kid, sometimes my legs would ache until my mother massaged away the pain. "They're just growing pains, honey," she would tell me. "This discomfort is actually helping you grow." At the time, Mom was only referring to the physical part of life, but of course, there is a spiritual application to her words. Whenever you and I face pain, we can be sure it's an opportunity for growth. God's purpose for us is not to make us happy or healthy or wealthy, although none of those things is inherently bad. His agenda involves a worthier aim—that of making us more like Christ. Romans 8:29 sums it up well: "For those whom he foreknew he also predestined to be conformed to the image of his Son...." On good days and bad, in sunshine and in rain, that is God's goal for us.

The apostle Paul had a thorn in the flesh that is never really defined in Scripture. It could have been a physical illness or infirmity, or maybe it was an emotional struggle of some sort. Whatever it was, it bothered Paul. In fact, he asked God three times to remove that thorn, but each time, God said no. More specifically, God said in reply, "My grace is sufficient for you, for my power is made perfect in weakness" (2 Corinthians 12:9). God is strongest when His children are weak.

Those opportunities for weakness, James says, equate to

the testing or purifying of our faith. And just as a furnace refines gold, the heat of our pain and discomfort can actually yield valuable results in the end.

The epic story of Job is well-known. He's the guy who lost everything, thanks to Satan garnering permission from God to have a heyday in Job's life. His health, his wealth, his family, and his sense of mental well-being—all of these things were taken from Job, and upon seeing his desperate situation, Job's wife gave him some advice. "Why don't you just curse God and die?" she suggested, which I find terribly ironic. God allowed nearly everything to be taken from Job but left him one crazy wife! Even so, Job refused to give in. I'm sure he doubted God's purposes for the devastation Job had endured, but in response to his wife's recommendation, Job simply said, "Though he slay me, I will hope in him" (Job 13:15).

> **His health, his wealth, his family, and his sense of mental well-being—all of these things were taken from Job...**

"My health can deteriorate. My wealth can dissipate. My friends can all walk out. And yet *still* I will trust in the Lord." The declaration was certainly true of Job; I wonder if it's true of us, too. Just after Satan was allowed to take Job's property and children, he tore his robe, he shaved his head, and he fell to the ground and worshipped God. "Naked I came from my mother's womb, and naked shall I return," he said. "The LORD gave, and the LORD has taken away; blessed be the name of the LORD" (Job 1:21). These days, we sing that magnificent praise chorus, "Blessed be the Name of the Lord." May we always mean the words that we sing.

Although I never would have chosen for my father to die so early in his life, I can say today that I am grateful for the suffering I endured. In my weakness, God really was made strong. And as I looked to Him to guide me, not only was my own faith enriched, but I was able to help strengthen the faith of others. When you and I walk through a fiery furnace and by God's grace make it to the other side in one piece, we become credible teachers who can help others learn to do the same. Our pain often serves as a pulpit from which we broadcast God's great love. It really is true: when the world sees us endure deep heartache while still insisting on trusting God, they come away saying, "Whatever you have is *exactly* what I need!"

Our pain often serves as a pulpit from which we broadcast God's great love.

"Be steadfast, immovable, always abounding in the work

of the Lord," 1 Corinthians 15:58 says, "knowing that in the Lord your labor is not in vain." In other words: don't give up; don't give in; keep going until the very end! American icon Hubert Humphrey summed up this idea well. He was a politician and a patriot and had boundless energy and optimism throughout his life. Following cancer surgery, he was given only a slim chance to live. But upon hearing a friend express sympathy for his plight, instead of wallowing in his troubles, Humphrey said, "Oh, my friend, it isn't what they take from you that counts; it is what you do with what you have left!" What is left for us *always* includes the grace and love of God. Regardless of what is taken from you in this life, never doubt the faithfulness of God.

Promise #3: "I'll give you the crown of life."

I mentioned earlier that I found three divine promises to help me overcome my darkest, doubt-filled days. In addition to being reassured that I have access to God's wisdom and that He stands ready to exchange my doubt with faith, He reminded me that the reward for persevering through pain is a crown of life someday.

In 1 Samuel 30, we find David and his band of men in the lowest emotional valley they'd known. They had just returned to their home city to find it had been pillaged and burned to the ground by a warring tribe of people. Their wives and children had been taken captive, and as they surveyed the bleak scene that once bustled with vibrancy and life, they wept. They were desperate and told God so. Thankfully, He intervened.

Verse 6 says that David "strengthened himself in the LORD his God," and then, ten verses later, we see David and his men eating and drinking and dancing, in celebration of God returning to them all that had been lost. "David recovered all that the Amalekites had taken," the text then says, "and David rescued his two wives. Nothing was missing, whether small or great, sons or daughters, spoil or anything that had been taken. David brought back all" (v. 18). Light overcame the darkness; faith overshadowed their doubts. There is a lesson here for us today.

I don't know if God will restore to us everything we have lost in this life—I won't see my dad again, for instance, until I get to heaven. But what I do know is that someday you and I will receive crowns for the crucibles we face. "Blessed is the man who remains steadfast under trial," James 1:12 promises, "for when he has stood the test he will receive the crown of life, which God has promised to those who love him." There will be a crown of rejoicing when we get to heaven, but there is another crown for the here and now. Psalm 103:4 says that as we go about our daily lives, God crowns us with mercy and love. It is that present-tense promise we must remember, when we face overwhelming darkness and doubt. We must remember what the apostle Paul knew to be true, that "the sufferings of this present time are not worth comparing with the glory that is to be revealed to us" (Romans 8:18). In other words, the agonizing labor pains our entire planet feels now will someday be resolved. Things will be redeemed. Things will be restored. Things will finally be set right. This is the reality we hope for, the future for which we wait.

In the meantime, we take our uncertainties and worries and doubts directly to the foot of the Cross. We bring God our heartfelt whys, knowing that He is big enough to handle them and small enough to care. We rest in the wisdom He offers His children, and we thank Him for hearing our cries. We remember that even Jesus experienced doubt in his life, when from the Cross He asked His heavenly Father, "Why have you forsaken me?" (Matthew 27:46). But it was this same Christ who endured suffering without despising it and, three days later, rose from the grave to prove God's faithfulness always prevails. And with firsthand knowledge to bear it out, He said, "In this world you will have tribulation, but take heart; I have overcome the world" (John 16:33).

Because of Jesus' sacrifice on the Cross that day, wisdom can replace our whys, faith can replace our doubts, and the crown of life we are promised can enrich every day that we live. We can live as *overcomers*, regardless of the challenges we face.

※

George Matheson was a nineteenth-century Scottish theologian and preacher who seemed destined for greatness. He was engaged to be married to a beautiful young woman, until his fiancée learned that he was going blind and told him she could not go through life with a blind man and abruptly broke off the engagement. Matheson took the news hard.

Years later, Matheson attended his sister's wedding, where he was hit afresh with his painful reality: he was blind, broken-hearted, and alone. But in the midst of that emotional rainstorm, God painted a rainbow in the sky. It came in the form of a hymn that we still sing in churches today. "O Love That Wilt Not Let Me Go" took Matheson less than five minutes to write, but the comfort it afforded his heart lasted until his dying day. See if the following lyrics encourage you in similar ways:

> O Love that wilt not let me go
> I rest my weary soul in thee;
> I give thee back the life I owe
> That in thine ocean depths its flow
> May richer, fuller be.
>
> O light that foll'west all my way
> I yield my flick'ring torch to thee;
> My heart restores its borrowed ray
> That in thy sunshine's blaze its day
> May brighter, fairer be.
>
> O Joy that seekest me through pain
> I cannot close my heart to thee;
> I trace the rainbow through the rain
> And feel the promise is not vain,
> That morn shall tearless be.
>
> O Cross that liftest up my head
> I dare not ask to fly from thee;

I lay in dust life's glory dead
And from the ground there blossoms red
Life that shall endless be.[5]

The third stanza is moving to me, the idea of joy seeking us out, even in the midst of the pain that we endure. Twenty years after my father's death, I went with a prison-ministry team to the penitentiary where the man who took my father's life was serving a life sentence. Our purpose for visiting that day was to share the Gospel with as many inmates as possible, and I couldn't help but wonder what I would do if he and I came face to face. As soon as the thought crossed my mind, I vowed before God that if the meeting somehow occurred, I would share the Good News of Christ's redemption and restoration with him. I would tell him that God loves him and that if he chose to surrender his life to His heavenly Father, nothing would ever separate him from that love—not past failings. Not present doubts. Not *anything*.

God did not orchestrate the meeting that day. But perhaps equally important, He brought about the realization in my mind and heart that I really had forgiven the man who ushered in so much pain for my family and me. Over the years, joy had sought me out and found me, and as a result, I had overcome.

---

[5] O, Love That Will Not Let Me Go, George Matheson, 1882. Public Domain.

I don't know the level of pain you face today, but I assure you that right in the midst of it, *joy* is seeking you out. The God who knit you together in your mother's womb wants to relate to you as an intimate friend. He wants to walk with you, talk with you, and experience all of life by your side. He wants to infuse your days with great joy. I know it's tough when the storm clouds gather not to fret or fear or doubt. But it is then that we can request from God that rainbow in the rain. Lay down your last concern, my friend, and let the God of all creation show you His care.

He wants to infuse your days with great joy.

)(

Please call 1-800-414-7693 to order the following products:

BOOKS:
A Man of God
Are you Fit for Life?
Courageous Parenting
Life According to Jesus
Lessons from the Heart
A Hope and a Future
Powering Up
Triumph! How You Can Overcome Death and Gain Eternal Life
The Promise of Persistent Prayer

DEVOTIONALS:
A Daily Encounter with God

BOOKLETS:
30 Days to Powerful Prayer
The Truth About Influence
True Womanhood
New Life in Christ
Rock Solid
Pause: Resting In God Instead of Stressing Out
Lifebook: The Authority, Authenticity and Accuracy of God's Word

G R A H A M

1-800-414-7693 (1-800-414-POWER)
jgraham@powerpoint.org
jackgraham.org